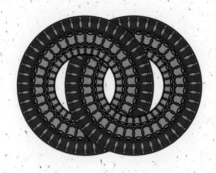

WITHOUT WINGS

WITHOUT WINGS

LAURIE LAMON

POETRY

CavanKerry ◈ Press LTD.

Library of Congress Cataloging-in-Publication Data
Lamon, Laurie, 1956–
Without wings : poems / by Laurie Lamon.
p. cm.
ISBN-13: 978-1-933880-12-9
ISBN-10: 1-933880-12-0
I. Title.

PS3612.A5474W58 2009
811'.6–dc22

2009009400

Cover art, Kicking Rocks, Joseph Hart © 2006
Author photograph by Jordan Huotari
Cover and book design by Peter Cusack

First Edition 2009
Printed in the United States of America

CavanKerry Press Ltd.
Fort Lee, New Jersey
www.cavankerrypress.org

FSC
Mixed Sources
Product group from well-managed
forests, controlled sources and
recycled wood or fiber

Cert no. SW-COC-002283
www.fsc.org
© 1996 Forest Stewardship Council

NOTABLE VOICES
CavanKerry❖Press

CavanKerry Press is proud to publish the works
of established poets of merit and distinction.

NEW JERSEY
STATE COUNCIL
ON THE ARTS

Discover
JERSEY
ARTS

CavanKerry Press is grateful for the
support it receives from the
New Jersey State Council on the Arts.

the small boat was leaving,
they were burning the newspapers in a straw hat
in the middle of the water.

—Yannos Ritsos, from "What's the Use?"

*

If I were an angel, before I turned around
I would be too weary to fly with my wings.

—Yehuda Amichai from "My Son Was Drafted"

*

Many waters cannot quench love,
neither can the floods drown it.

—Song of Solomon 8:7

CONTENTS

three

for William

§

Pain Thinks of a Word

the tongue without sweetness & broken
the cup the fields of Assisi

forsaken & dark & light without
praise Pain thinks of a word forsaken

the body the *mare undarum*
the waves *the tongue without sweetness*

Pain thinks of the body the hands
& feet without praise the field a word

forsaken Pain thinks of a word
& light & dark the cup the red poppy

Pain Thinks of Heaven & Earth

Pain thinks of flame willow
the vowel & tongue
the body's palm & neural arch

Pain thinks of the earth
beneath wind the hemisphere
without sound Pain thinks

of heaven the fallen darkness
& light the unforsaken
planets vanquished & visible

Pain Thinks of Something Biography

what it was without growing old a fever .
a checkup the cold front dragging
a rake a plow Pain thinks of something

biography a place a word clearing &
threshing snow & leaves opening the hour
without growing old what it was Pain

thinks of something arthritis colloquy
of field & figure light what it was without
blindness Pain thinks of something

biography what house & table
without growing old without *habitude*
without *offering* what evidence taking its meat

Pain Thinks of Alcibiades

Pain thinks of the sea the blackened
fields the shore without daylight
Pain thinks of the hour's fires without
witness the horses breaking & the sea
breaking Pain thinks of the fields the tide
rising in light's black zone without body
or breath Pain thinks of the sea without
witness Pain thinks of Alcibiades

one

Look How Far You've Come

I gave you a tree
and you said *tree*
and then cut and cut
until you were
hoarse with calling
back the rings
back the branches.
I gave you wind
and you thought it
was a box a sheet
something to cart away
all you had burned.
I gave you land
and you dug a pit
a canal you dug stone
from a quarry
and now look
look at the statues
one by one how
they resemble you.

No

The dog lay on the wet porch and watched
as I dragged the shovel and rake across the yard,

as I began to dig up the sod of an old bed
and the rocks and lost bones he would have carried

into a corner and chewed quietly until I noticed,
telling him *no*, pulling the mass from his jaws.

Time to come in, you called from the doorway,
seeing the mound of vines and roots whose sterilized

inches of soil I broke open twenty years ago
without pause to read what water, temperature,

and hemispheric zone would be required
for maximum growth. *Time to come in*, you called

again, darkness gathering in the gradual way
we understand need: nothing at the beginning.

Thinking of Beauty, Thinking of Truth

One sees the color that belies the field.
One sees that the field is brown or blue as an eye
or a body of water, and without love
or hatred beneath a cloudless sky. Seeing
the water, one thinks of truth: flowers changed
from rosette to leaf and stalk, and then
sheaths of brown beneath snow, and then snow
blankness covering stones where footprints
might be seen the way wings caught
in a web are flight suspended by weight.
Thinking of beauty, thinking of truth,
one walks between field and sky, and self
is dissolved between word and thought.
One walks to be visible. One chooses the white.

Heaven

we marveled
at the bathroom tile and the retractable
clothesline, the bedroom window's iron grille

whose nails, driven into brick, had pulled
loose and held through decades
of rust and wind, world wars, a thousand

thousand burning sunset hours. We watched
dusk flame against the window ledge
where our sack of cold food stayed cold,

and where the pigeons we named Edward
and Sophia had basked, their pearl gray breasts
pulsing with the ordinary blood

of mates alighting in a narrow space
inside a view's corridor—wind and cage of wind
swung above the street like a painting on a nail.

Unsettled, they carried upward
their feathers' ladders of dirt and air, and met
the evening's narrow crosshatched

winds, their bodies laden with the small exegeses
we imagined to be thirst and hunger,
hunger and gladness.

We had turned our chairs to watch through flecks
of paint and faded fingerprints the street,
the rooms across from us—in daylight, a woman's back,

a blue-white hinge of desk and window,
the sweater draped across a chair
and falling earthward—an abundant, pale yellow.

Mountain Ash

1

A friend has told me she cannot live
the way the medication leaves her without

her mind that has always looked to this season's
turning of light—dusk arriving through rain,

and the rain meeting a dry riverbed which all summer
drew deer nearer her watered lawn.

She tells me she is living in the space before
a canvas and looking to see where tremors end.

2

I pulled them from the rake as you moved the ladder
and climbed to cut more branches—

scraped against the ground, the berries were
the color of fire and air torn by fire.

I held the split leaves and thought of a rope pulling
a bell, and the sound of the bell moving

earthward, reaching the body, the temporary mask,
and the mask tearing in two.

Sunday at Port-en-Bessin 1888, Georges Seurat

We moved through the gallery rooms past the exact
moment when the woman would have awakened
and slipped her feet into sandals and then broken open
the seal of rain which veiled the window, seeing
the gloves left last night on the wooden bench, and farther,
the small dog turned to the spray hitting the jetty,
not having heard the command to stay but continuing
to run as he had run yesterday—to have the light
to himself, the waves and the scent of seawater, yellow,
blue, and black, these colors for himself—and the pour
of wind and the sea rim moving and not moving
against the jetty like the heart pounding, pounding.

I've Stopped Staying Up Late to Write Poems

I'm forcing myself to get up early, to shake
off these dreams, the syllables round-mouthed
as the veins of trees and the clamor of water
traveling upward, thousands of miles—
I'm forgetting sex, the mother and father,
mythology, the ancient ponds. I'm forgetting
weaponry and gardens, continents
of endangered beak and claw, the bedroom
waterfalls and basement floors where children
watch for signs of redemption. Earlier
and earlier I'm refusing the psalms of the dark;
I'm recanting my allegiances. As for memory,
it died in a forest. I forget the ache of cold.
I forget the snow where I buried its clothes.

The Angel

was tired of travel, bored
with the millennia's airy
hue, and wings everywhere
opening like baby grands.
It watched as a crushed

cup floated at the pond
edge where we crouched,
fanning bread across cloud
and sunspots, the green
shadows of rocks beneath

a green-gold island.
The angel watched the island,
the willow and swan nest,
and the animals in between
the rain-pale cygnets

and the adults whose necks
were dark with feeding
and whose feet were black,
not yellow like the sun drawn
by this year's schoolchildren.

Description

The edge of the house was white
and green, an edge of trees
like a hand beneath a book

holding the book to the light.
The edge of the house was an edge
of the roof that was white

where snow had fallen and lay
in one place, a description
of snow tilted up toward light,

an angle that was
a description of light and dark
seen in one place.

The house was a description
undisturbed, seen from a window
where, in sunlight, snow

was gathering and breaking,
drops falling on the dark green
leaves of rhododendron.

Beyond the green, a woman
had come out of the house.
She was wearing white and beige.

The purse was red,
red that was becoming unmoored,
slow, a thought of red

that had never been cast in speech—
not a word before now,
not the ordinary stagger and sight.

to Know

*to recognize as being the same as something
previously known.*
                    —*Webster's New Collegiate*

I didn't know how many miles we are
        from the earth's center
        (*3,000 miles*),

or the diameter of the earth's core
        (*3/4ths that of the moon*),
        or that every 400 years the earth's inner-

core is a full turn
        ahead of the surface where I
        am reading in bed, upright as a coin

spun on a table, an illustration
        of goodwill between acceleration
        and gravity whose laws have landed us

here, on a mattress resting above an aged
        hardwood floor. The edges
        of oak drift and touch like fold

or tear faults we silence
        occasionally with nails driven
        up from the basement where coolness

has collected for years like the heart's
        faith and doubt.
        Beyond the window, bees

are drawn to the rhododendron
      and coreopsis, hues we cannot
      see, nor the mouth parts sensitive to heat,

nor the feathery leg hairs raddled
      with pollen. To tell where more food is, they
      dance in the hive. What sways

with ripeness they find by knowing light's
      immeasurable season—for them,
      sweetness offered like strokes of luck.

Light we don't know how to know
      finds us: mornings before
      we are fully awake when you draw

my leg across you and cup
      my foot, and then the ankle bone your fingers
      circle as though it were a city on a map,

or evening,
      when we watch the bird coming
      not for water.
            Closer.

Reading the Poem

smell of clay, the rim
of sky unable to close
weight's leaf edge—

light against a wall,
a cup, crease of porcelain
slip, mouth and eye

reading the poem, lines
of table and cloth,
the hour in the distance

where everything was
meant: the wall
where there is shade,

the tree where there is shade,
fruit, bread,
likeness—

reading the poem,
instant light, instant
water, consonants, irises

irises.

When You Say Yes

Let it be on a Thursday or a Sunday
evening between the hours of 6

and 8, or in the morning when children
are standing on street corners

waiting for a bus and the young ones
are held by the hand and the older ones

are holding hands for the first time.
Let there be a man walking past in a blue

Windbreaker, and let the dog pulling
at her lead be at the beginning of her life.

When you say yes, let it be on a Monday
or a Friday, and let there be candles

at the edge of a pier and couples dancing;
let there be old and new green

along the river where you slow to watch
for the heron who sometimes is there,

and because of a sound or a glimpse
of your faces, let it lift its long body

slowly, at an angle, the legs lingering
at first until the wings catch the air.

for Luke and Jana Lamon

§

Pain Thinks of the Pale of Settlement

Pain thinks of the eyes open
& closed the forehead's dust the mouth
open and closed Pain thinks

of the arm the leg numb as soil
the breasts numb as soil Pain thinks
of ankle & wrist the shoulder

the palm spacious as milk
Pain thinks of the body's temple &
throat the fingers crowded

with repetition Pain thinks
of pedestal & ditch the extinguished
gaze the shoe the star

Pain thinks of the pale of settlement
the arid cloth the dirt
pointing away from the heart.

Pain Thinks of the Angel

without waiting without memory
of waiting without history closing
its eyes Pain thinks of the angel
without fluency & hunger nothing
of rapture nothing of the table

Pain Thinks of Wind

without radiance pressing a window's
glass searching the neck the wrist for name
& address searching the back of an ear
the fingertip & nail the metal stem Pain
thinks of wind without helix & auricle
without first & last half light without
morning without the beginning or end
of morning Pain thinks of wind without
light without inch of glass without air
return without sound the cochlea's
wall Pain thinks of a window the wind
the miniature gold scroll pressed to the ear

Pain Thinks of Death

without sound the extant
waves *grotto & linden*
without trespass the mind
without evidence a voice
the eye nothing of light's
poverty Pan thinks of death
without poverty without
tenor a word's infinite space
the breath crowding in

two

Anne Frank Exhibit

a sign above the bed instructs us to imagine sleeping
here without name without detail's thread without
weight the stairway's one direction waking soundless
shoulder to shoulder looking through the curtain's hole
sized for watching the street where people are talking
are holding things crossing the river's blue-gray water
whose banks are green are bare of wind carrying
rain or snow against glass lifting dust to a windowsill
a fingerprint in the next room my husband and I hear
the murmur of voices an automobile a piano chord
the book pulled from a shelf & pages falling open *rain
snow* falling on a field dug open burned open soil &
root the word *breath* breath without transfer held here

Prime Number

It looks like a man wearing a shawl whose body is
another shawl wrapped around a man who has already
gone to his death in a subway, an office building,
a chair beside a hospital bed—a man leaning against
a lectern, or rising from a seat on a train that is leaving a city
for another city; it looks like sunrise or midnight; it looks
like prayer or hunger whose table and chair is without
company, without the forgiveness of bread and meat;

it looks like a woman sitting on a bus where two dozen
are seated at an intersection where nothing is meant
to keep from occurring; where nothing is meant to return
the explosion to the briefcase of work at her feet,
the weight of the sweater whose sleeves cross her breasts
to the dark emptiness of the body's withdrawal—
shoulder and arm, the wrist and palm's volume of light:
time that crosses the body's corridor, the eye's division.

The Beginning and the End

What do we make of the God of vengeance, the bloodshed of kings,
        the women running from homes without
preparation; what do we make at the end of astonishment's
        glance without preparation for darkness, and afterward,
darkness? What do we make of the landscape where stone begat stone,
        where soil was lifted and carried, and the cell's
transparency was lifted and carried; what do we make of the feathers,
        the imprint of glass, the black weather swept
into floorboards; what do we make of the twenty-seven bones
        of the hand, the clod of dirt, the ring?
What do we make of the son replacing his meals with mourning,
        his evening run and the hour of bedtime reading
with mourning? What do we make of a father's wristwatch, a hospital
        window, sun-splintered; what do we make
of the driver's license and telephone number, the heart's
        empty quarter, the history of voices, birthplace and geography,
the blurred eye, the shoelace pulled from the shoe?

The Falling

This hour primates are being injected with smallpox in doses millions of times
larger than that which would infect a human being: *accuracy*:   beneath rain a shore
sliding into the sea: a centerpiece weighted with stem and gravel: the splintered
cells of iris and orchid: *smaller*:   a blade width slicing a shark's dorsal fin: light's
corridor without brightness: 100 million sharks in one year: *smaller*:   the width
of an eyelid sealed during hunting and feeding: the retina's capacity for the
differentiation of colors: *accuracy*:   a needle's hollow tip touching the skin's site:
rain: the blue-green eyes of the deepwater shark: *smaller*:   droplets
wiped from the hand the nose the mouth: particles of light separating object
from darkness: *accuracy*:   beneath rain the earth jutting into the sea: the eye's
capacity for imprint of outline: the falling: *smaller*: the hour meeting the animals

Cerberus

It was the fifth day after New Year's day
that I recognized the dog in the bedroom—
sand-colored and still, an observant
of interior regions: Chaos and Erebus,
Aether and Hemera. And when at dawn

a light appeared again on the wall,
I knew it entered through the inch of space
that separated window from blind—a reflection
I had watched settle and waver. I knew
it was not illness or mystery that made me

see the dog halt in the doorway, sniffing
the humidified air before climbing onto the bed
where, like Cerberus, having seen enough,
he twisted and licked his pale legs
even into sleep.

Rice

I ask your husband where you are, noticing his soiled clothes,
thinking you have been working together in the orchard; I ask him
where I can find you, both of us speaking your name, *Alma*,
and the orchard behind us where you and I have filled boxes with plums
and carried them into the kitchen, and rinsed the clouded skins.

Behind him I can see the geraniums you dig up and carry
into the mudroom each autumn, bracing the stems against the wall
where he held you by the throat, where you saw the hallway
and the rooms behind him resembling sunlight, resembling the black
centers of irises, and the porcelain vase your mother carried

from Tehran. When you stood up, not feeling your hands,
when you stood up and walked to the kitchen and turned on the tap
and waited for cold water, you remembered how your mother
would pour water into a pan, and then rice—you noticed
the counter's half-inch tiles beneath your fingers bearing your weight.

You remembered that the water your mother
stirred was the color of milk you tasted this morning
and poured down the drain, neither you nor your husband
seeing the houseplants or the halos of dust—
not seeing the orchard through the kitchen window.

When you held one and then the other hand
beneath water, it was as if you remembered the nights
you had slept on the roof, and the way your mother
would bring a cold cloth to your skin. Through the netting
you watched the moon rise, and saw that it resembled nothing.

for Alma

Bonsai

Watering the maple,
I waited and listened for the soil
to take the stream I poured
across the black gravel
we spread with a spoon, making
a river, and a river
bend.

In the late light falling
across the garden, the petals
of the begonia are as translucent
as the skin of the infants
zipped into the carriages their mothers
push with one hand as they run
each morning, entering and leaving
the window's view.

There are three new leaves
we had not noticed.
They do not tremble against my finger.
They have not risen up
against a single wind, nor have they
taken in the clangorous rain.
Their silence is set apart
from the falling and tearing down
that is not yet the earth.

Dust

What is this sweater of air
breath unknits,

particle and light
the body wears, traveling

or standing still,
trapping inch of earth

and wind the eye feels
first, lashing shut?

Descended, it assumes
a daily shape—

bed and chair,
clock and candlewick,

the dog's lead pulled
by gravity and dog—

the silhouette
of every autumn's coat

dissolved by time
light wears to death

the body cannot feel even
then, meeting it at birth.

§

Pain Thinks of Eschatology

the hillside tomb broken and stripped beneath stone
against stone Pain reads turning the page every
corridor broken the fracture and tongue the obelus
broken without season of light without darkness
buried as the hour is buried without dedication
or season Pain reads without trace without gather
of light and the tomb without stone

Pain Thinks of the Deaf Dog the Subject

wants to touch the dog beaten nearly to death
the gaze the mouth tunnel it fled Pain thinks
of the photogene the deaf dog the blue

& white eye *in the dream the subject asks is*
benevolence *a word* the hand traveling the stilled
back & skull coat tight as breath Pain

thinks of the deaf dog the subject word &
phoneme stick harness *it is a word* Pain thinks
of the subject trained the body trained

the gaze open & closed the word's current
& shutter Pain thinks of the deaf dog the subject
Pain thinks of the blue the white eye

Pain Thinks of the Body

While the earth remaineth . . .
      —Genesis 8:22

Pain thinks of the body without waiting without
physics genetics barrage & ration the sea's
ellipses & cell while the earth remains Pain thinks
of the body the ark without gather's division
without frequency's wave & dust without outline
without witness Pain thinks of the body the sea
& light unharnessed the waves unharnessed

Pain thinks of the body the ark without raiment
the hour without gather's division the umbral
slant uncovered the solar corona the ark the path
of totality Pain thinks of the hour the outline
& light unharnessed the waves unharnessed the body
without witness & dark & light without waiting
the earth without waiting without gather's division

Pain Thinks of a Window

in thy light shall we see light.
   —Psalms 36:9

if light if a season of light if dark
if a season Pain thinks of a threshold
a psalm of return *the coat worn a single night*
Pain thinks of a window an orchard
& wreaths of smoke & sugar
if harvest & grain if light if a season
Pain thinks of a window *if peace if resistance*
apotheosis for the living a chime
for the living *the coat worn a single night*
for the dead a handrail & familiar
the infinite wood Pain thinks of a window
a psalm & anonymous the season
& torn the place of departure

three

Dragonfly

Its arrival was stillness
narrow as a hairpin, and the wings'
stigmas lain open, and
the eyes, yes, bezel green
and gold and blue, and the wide
mouth not without ambition,
waiting and drinking.

Instruction

I moved to the place
in the garden where we had been working
and waited   *a foot to the left   back*

a step   now another   as in the child's game
of surprise, blindfolds,
as in the adult game of temporary

forgiveness   *close your eyes*
what do you hear   feel   what weight against
your palm   what do you think

it is
presence like matter's gravity,
a boundary's weightlessness, balance as if

counterpoise,
as if the hand's own summoning   *come closer*
as if waves   *close your eyes*

and a child crouched
behind the blue cardboard, slowly
moving across a boundary's stage, seeing

the adult
world through the eyehole
slowly   *look up*   where the sky is complete

illusion and the shape of a tree
is a dome, silver-green, the convex curve's
trick of light

light's continuous motion,
as though the tree were not between seeing
and the plenitude of will

attenuated to this
recognition: it was grass and root knuckled
against branches, and then the dun

underside of feathers, a pale bloodshot
beak and the eye ringed with dust,
the body

held against the sky   *look up*
what do you see   that it was brightness given
without falling, without separation.

When

After Kevin Kramer's sled hit the tree
that broke his neck, he said the numbness
wasn't like the cold brought by needles,

or the burning waking brings to the arm
still asleep. It was something else of feeling
and adjacency, something else of earth

and snow—transparency the mind could
not replicate afterward, even when it dreamed
and woke the body falling, from falling.

The Dog

Getting up
in the dark,
I kick

the rawhide
knuckle
into

a corner,
step over
the sock

chewed
clean
as after

birth.
The dog
fogs

the window,
laps the view
of street

and shrubbery
growing
vaster,

darker—
howling,
hearing sirens

terrifying
trees,
he drags

unto himself
what he learned
to love—

the sock,
the shoe,
the hand he bites

in bed
where being
held is not

enough—
he wants
our skin to taste

like dirt;
he wants the air
to feel like fur.

Bridge

My father considers
the distance from the bridge to the wall
of a shed, the heat softened slats

where as a child he watched
wild horses, trying to be quiet, trying
not to think of the word *horses*

or a word for the soil
thick as sugar that circled their eyes.
Beneath the planks,

figures of water
and stone, and the currents
raising the stones

and setting them down, indelible
the wind and indelible the water shadowed
by footprints. My father

considers dividing the bridge
into sections as though it were land.
He considers the distance between the shed

and the horses
who are breaking the sod,
who are eating the inside from the outside.

for Karl Lamon

To a Brother

Think, how we held out
     money for the ice cream
          melting and freezing in waxed

sheathes, the shims of milk and sherbet
     stacked, candlelike,
          their wooden sticks damp

and blurred. The street and yards
     were sunstruck where we wondered
          at our shadows made

visible—
     think of the brightening—
          as with the ground's featurelessness

passed over,
     and the men and the animals
          traveling *in solstitio brumali.*

Abeyance

You were wearing a new leather coat. Your new wife stayed to watch
TV in a motel room twenty yards from the Clark Fork River.
It was the end of the honeymoon, you said, the end of the money.

You told me you'd loved my mother since she was fifteen for her
brown eyes and the black hair she finally cut when she turned thirty,
when already there was no place where you could speak to her.

Then, driving overnight loads, every road meant the startled dawn
of birds rising from wheat or ditch. In a same sudden light
twenty years ago, you lay before me in a viewing room, and I

tried to see the certainty of your mouth and fist. I folded
a note into your suit pocket, believing in the imperishable. That winter,
driving past the house where your parents had lived for forty years,

I glimpsed the frozen lake through trees lining the shore road where
thirty years ago my brother and I had walked for miles to call our mother.
Returning, we found the house with flashlights, and you waiting.

All evening you had watched your father rock on his hands and knees
as you told him to keep breathing, neither of you seeing the light at the lake's
edge or hearing the animals traveling through the yard. When you saw

that he'd had enough, you kicked the furniture out of the way
and got down beside him and rocked and breathed and told him to stop
fucking around. Afterward you lay beside him on the floor, pressed

against the one place you knew he could abide without anger or fear
the way a field, laying beneath snow, without memory of acquiescence, holds
the imprint of our angel shape, shallow and cold and without wings.

for John Lamon

Poem for a Friend

I opened the door
for the dogs and felt
their small travel
across the threshold
· pause against my legs
when they met their
own familiar scent—

there is no place we
find where the body
lets go without
witness: the eye when
we sleep sees the shape
being was used to—
not blindness
but sound and presence
coming near,
and the boy and
the girl letting it come,
and the hands open.

for Marty Erb

Painting the Kitchen

When I removed the outlet cover, dead bees fell onto the sugar
        and coffee canisters, fell into the toaster.
                The counter was covered

with bodies, black and gold—the wall's tomb stacked with more
        bees. Inexplicable, the humming I had heard for
                months, opening a cupboard or turning off water,

not remembering the bees I had found last summer
        on the basement floor and windowsills, cold and drowsed—
                for months, bees flying up the stairs

to the back door window fogged with light. What scent or
        vibration had they known to follow, tunneling all summer
                through a wall's interior?

Standing at the counter, slicing bread or pouring
        wine, I had not heard them crawling in, hovering
                and massed, historical and small as a hand on a door.

I scraped what remains I could see with a screwdriver
        onto the counter and examined the papery shreds. The dead were
                weightless as my hand beneath water

cleaning the paintbrush, pushing the spattered
        handle down against the bristles, watching as tap water
                lifted the paint and pooled in the sink, opaque as milk poured

and rinsed from a glass. I passed the brush back and forth
        beneath the stream contiguous and clear as the corridor
                the bees had crawled through toward our

sound and motion. We must have become as familiar
       as light to shade—ourselves the season's end the bees flew toward
          like blossoms falling, loosened late into air.

Forgetting the Water Poem

I didn't want to wake you.
I had already gotten up from bed
once for something I wanted to remember.

I had been holding your arm in the crook
of my arm; your sleep was shallow.
You were not dreaming. Your face

was like the face of a child who is reading,
or looking at a watch.
And the dog was asleep beside us

on the bed we had made where you
could reach down
and touch him with your fingers

when he yelped and ran in the dream
of running. There is nothing I remember
of the water poem I wanted

to keep, while the nothing of forgetting
widened and darkness was
what it was.

You were sleeping.
I didn't want to wake you. In the morning
we saw that it had snowed.

The view was a vast whiteness
narrowed by trees and yards. The night glasses
of water when I poured them out

were full and cold.

We had not touched them to our mouths.

We had not left fingerprints.

Last Words

Are without amend,
without darkness and light's

caesura and awl. Are dumb
as the moon commencing another

emptiness, the lunar eyes
and mouth like the flooded caves

whose waters wear against
the outline of animals painted there

in silence, in the fire-
scored light that blackened the walls.

Bird Call, Wave

Wife, my husband
said. *Husband.* The ocean

through the shades, motion
and light—the near call

of the bird we had begun to call
the 4 o'clock bird.

Then something else when I opened
my hand and turned

to the window side of the bed
where he had moved,

having drawn the sheet, cold
and welcome, across my shoulders.

Better to hear the waves.
Better the bird's cry

released the way a spondee's
struck sound is meant

to be given and given—not sweat
and mouth. Not the orchid

farmed and cut. No sound but the bird
and the sea, and no bird

alone but eye to eye. And then the praise
that was the sea. And then the wings.

Acknowledgments

I am greatly indebted to the Artist Trust/Washington State Arts Commission for a fellowship that supported the time during which many of these poems were written; and to Whitworth University and the Weyerhaeuser Center for Faith and Learning for their support. I am indebted to my colleagues and students, and my family for their care and support. I remain deeply grateful to Donald Hall for his heart and his vision for both poet and poetry.

Thanks are due to the following publications for permission to reprint poems in this present volume: *Arts and Letters Journal of Contemporary Culture*: "Painting the Kitchen," "Cerberus," "Rice," "*No*," "Pain Thinks of the Deaf Dog the Subject," "Pain Thinks of a Word"; *The Colorado Review*: "Instruction"; *Northwest Review*: "Bird Call, Wave," "When"; *Pleiades*: "Pain Thinks of Eschatology"; *Ploughshares*: "Pain Thinks of Alcibiades," "Pain Thinks of Something Biography"; *Rock & Sling*: "To a Brother"; *The New Republic*: "Prime Number," "Pain Thinks of the Pale of Settlement," "Pain Thinks of the Body," "Pain Thinks of Wind"; *Tiferet*: "Dust"; *Willow Springs*: "Pain Thinks of the Angel."

For epigraphs on page ix: "My Son Was Drafted" in *Open Closed Open*, copyright © 2000 by Yehuda Amichai, English translation copyright © 2000 by Chana Bloch and Chana Kronfeld, reprinted by permission of Houghton Mifflin Harcourt Publishing Company.

Credit: Yannis Ritsos, "What's the Use?" translated by N. C. Germanacos, from *Selected Poems* 1939–1988, edited by Kimon Friar and Kostas Myrsiades. Translation copyright 1976 by N. C. Germanacos. Reprinted with the permission of BOA Editions, Ltd.

Other Books in the Notable Voices Series

An Apron Full of Beans, Sam Cornish

The Red Canoe: Love in Its Making, Jaon Cusack Handler

Bear, Karen Chase

The Poetry Life: Ten Stories, Baron Wormser

Fun Being Me, Jack Wiler

Common Life, Robert Cording

The Origins of Tragedy & other poems, Kenneth Rosen

Against Consolation, Robert Cording

Apparition Hill, Mary Ruefle

CavanKerry's Mission

Through publishing and programming, CavanKerry Press connects communities of writers with communities of readers. We publish poetry that reaches from the page to include the reader, by the finest new and established contemporary writers. Our programming brings our books and our poets to people where they live, cultivating new audiences and nourishing established ones.